D0339562

MAP WORKBOOK FOR
WORLD HISTORY

VOLUME I
THIRD EDITION

CYNTHIA KOSSO
NORTHERN ARIZONA UNIVERSITY

WADSWORTH

THOMSON LEARNING

Australia • Canada • Mexico • Singapore • Spain • United Kingdom • United States

COPYRIGHT © 2001 Wadsworth Group. Wadsworth, is an imprint of the Wadsworth Group, a division of Thomson Learning, Inc. Thomson Learning™ is a trademark used herein under license.

ALL RIGHTS RESERVED. No part of this work covered by the copyright hereon may be reproduced or used in any form or by any means—graphic, electronic, or mechanical, including photocopying, recording, taping, Web distribution, or information storage and retrieval systems—without the prior written permission of the publisher.

Printed in the United States of America

4 5 6 7 04 03 02

For permission to use material from this text, contact us by **Web:** http://www.thomsonrights.com **Fax:** 1-800-730-2215 **Phone:** 1-800-730-2214

ISBN 0-534-57179-4

For more information, contact
Wadsworth/Thomson Learning
10 Davis Drive
Belmont, CA 94002-3098
USA

For more information about our products, contact us:
Thomson Learning Academic Resource Center
1-800-423-0563
http://www.wadsworth.com

International Headquarters
Thomson Learning
International Division
290 Harbor Drive, 2nd Floor
Stamford, CT 06902-7477
USA

UK/Europe/Middle East/South Africa
Thomson Learning
Berkshire House
168-173 High Holborn
London WC1V 7AA
United Kingdom

Asia
Thomson Learning
60 Albert Complex, #15-01
Singapore 189969

Canada
Nelson Thomson Learning
1120 Birchmount Road
Toronto, Ontario M1K 5G4
Canada

Map Workbook for World History
VOLUME ONE
(to ca. 1600)

Contents

Introduction

Map reading is an important part of any person's basic knowledge, whether for travel or keeping track of events around the world. When someone gives you directions, or asks them of you, your brain automatically attempts to draw a rudimentary map. Your mind may even see roads as lines, rivers as bands, or buildings as small squares.

This world map workbook is designed to familiarize you with the natural and political geography of the world. My hope is that this book will enhance your understanding of the interconnectedness of the world that began essentially from the appearance of humans on earth. The modern world has been created not just by a few isolated (or noisy) cultures, but by the interactions among all the world's cultures throughout time. In the following pages you will find both map exercises and short-answer essay questions intended to help you understand the regions of the world in the broadest sense. Though there are brief introductions to each section, it is expected that you will have access to either a Western Civilization or World Civilization textbook, and a historical atlas.

Maps are, of course, useful for understanding history and geography. Maps tell us about the physical and cultural aspects of the world, but they can be deceiving. Colors and sizes can be used to subtly suggest "good guys" or "bad guys," or relative importance. For example, placing one's country in the middle of the map and larger than others around it helps emphasize the political and cultural importance of one's homeland. In addition, maps have had a very long and interesting history.

Brief History of Maps

Old maps and prints are fascinating because of their power to reflect the history of the world. When and where the very first maps were created is unknown. Clearly, as soon as symbols were used people felt the need to draw routes and illustrate their own territories. Among the earliest known maps is one found in Turkey (Anatolia) at the site of Çatal Hüyük, dating back to about 6300 BCE. This map, a wall painting, is a town plan, with a volcano looming in the background. Several thousand years later Egyptians, Assyrians and Babylonians also produced early maps and plans on papyrus and clay tablets. These were most likely land surveys for tax purposes. Controversy concerning the shape of the earth consumed philosophers, from Anaximander to Strabo. Determining the shape of the earth, its size, habitable areas, climate zones and relative positions of regions has preoccupied mapmakers over the centuries. Mathematicians, philosophers and astronomers all sought answers to these problems. Plato, Herodotus and Aristotle all thought the world was round, an idea that eventually took hold in the Hellenic world. From our point of view, Strabo plays an important role in preserving the story of early map developments, though he misinterpreted the calculations made by Eratosthenes and Posidonius concerning the circumference of the earth. His work, *Geography,* is preserved in eight books and reveals sound geographic understanding, and it also reveals an encyclopedic understanding of the countries and people of the Mediterranean region.

The Greek mathematician, Claudius Ptolemy, produced one of the most important early developments in map making. In ca. 150 CE, he collated all known information and created his *Geography* (also a work in eight volumes). This work became the basis of mapping for about the next 1000 years and influenced the mapmakers who provided maps for explorers such as Columbus, Cabot and Magellan. However, improvements in map making were slowed by the fall of the Roman Empire and the loss or dissipation of accumulated information. Increasing religious piety and the belief in a flat world forced the simplification of maps in Western Europe.

Following the Crusades, Westerners were reintroduced to Ptolemy's work, as well as the sophisticated mathematical knowledge of the Arabs, which influenced later medieval mapmakers. Greek manuscripts from Constantinople were also brought to the West, and once translated into Latin, these began to intrigue scholars of historical geography. It was only with the advent of printing, however, that the production of numerous copies of maps became possible. The "age of discovery" brought more than discoveries of new lands. New geometric methods of survey were also discovered, as well as the invention of much better instruments. Increasingly modern and recognizable (to us) maps were made. The Spanish and the Portuguese were particularly influential because of their fine, early maritime charts (though, of course at first these were kept very secret). In 1569, after advances in surveying technology had been made, the first Mercator maps were produced. As the quality of maps improved, they became art forms in their own right. These maps, though beautiful, still contained numerous inaccuracies (California, for example, was drawn as an island).

During the eighteenth century the demand for maps grew stronger, and middle class and aristocratic people alike collected atlases, maps, new books and similar luxuries. Many of these were huge folio maps, highly decorated. It was this elite market that began to demand more accuracy in map making, ultimately to the benefit of all. With the invention of steel engraving in the nineteenth century, mass production of maps became even easier. Maps were printed in large quantities and it was easier to keep them up to date. However, with an increase in accuracy, decoration became less common. Slowly, maps lost most of their decorative features—as can be seen in modern maps—such as those in this workbook and in your atlases and texts. Aerial photography and satellite surveying have helped to furnish a wealth of detail hitherto missing from maps, and these techniques have been used to enhance the accuracy and detail of all kinds of maps.

Defining Maps

Maps, in a way, are very simple. They are just geographic regions drawn on a flat surface. Typically there are a number of commonly accepted standards and symbols used by all modern mapmakers. These symbols are defined in the key. In order to make the map (or to read one) a frame of reference is chosen. A grid system within the frame of reference is usually used to help pinpoint locations on the map. Drawing the lines of latitude and longitude creates the grid, which helps to pinpoint locations accurately. Mapmakers chose the north and south poles as two definite, and less politically motivated, points from which to begin dividing up the world. Midway between these poles a line was drawn around the world (this is the equator). Next, lines were drawn parallel to the equator up and down to each of the poles (the lines of latitude). To complete the grid, lines were drawn from pole to pole (the lines of longitude).

While the equator provides a natural line from which to measure, there is no such natural longitude line (though one is put in by convention and is called the prime meridian). A longitudinal starting point is obviously needed as a point of reference. The line through Greenwich, England is now most commonly used, but many nations have created maps with their own most important cities as reference points. The United States made maps with Washington DC as the prime meridian. The Spanish drew their reference line through Madrid, the Greeks through Athens, the Dutch through Amsterdam, and so on.

Many different scales of maps are used, meaning simply that there are maps with different proportions between the distance on the map and the actual distance on the world. The larger the fraction (or proportion), the smaller the territory covered. Inches per mile or centimeters per kilometer are the most common kind of scale. The scale is merely a fraction comparing the measures on the map (inches or centimeters) with the measures on the ground (miles or kilometers).

Finding the exact location of any place requires several steps. Reproducing this location accurately is further complicated by one simple fact: the world is round and most maps are not. This fact of life leads to unavoidable distortion in the spatial representation of locations. (You may notice that the shapes of continents change slightly from map to map. This is because the distortion is different depending upon the perspective of the map.) Obviously, flat maps are not likely to be completely superseded by globes. Carrying a globe on a hike or road trip would be very inconvenient.

Map projections are the various ways in which one deals with the problem of distortion of the earth's surface on a map. The world is round (most people agree). The map page is flat. All mapmakers, therefore, pick a perspective and a scale from which to display their particular purpose or orientation. For a map nearly devoid of distortion one must have a spherical surface (this is known as a globe). Obviously, a flat map cannot perfectly represent a round surface. Typically a compromise is made whereby the directions, distances and areas are drawn with the least inaccuracy possible to each. The Mercator maps are an example of how this works. The Mercator projection is related to a cylindrical projection (where the mapmaker, or cartographer, works with the map as though it were a cylinder that circles the globe). Mercator maps do this, and thereby show the equator with great accuracy, while they distort the highest latitudes (this is known as the "Greenland problem" because of the difficulty of properly fitting Greenland, which is on the top or at the north of the map, in anything close to accurate proportions).

Map Perspectives

There are, as well, several kinds of maps. Political maps traditionally show territorial boundaries and political divisions. Hydrographic charts are used for navigation and show bodies of water and shores. Geologic maps show the physical structure of a region, while topographic maps show man made and natural surface features in given regions.

Every map, therefore, has a particular perspective. It has an author (the cartographer), a subject, and a theme. The subject in this exercise book is Western Civilization; themes vary from boundaries to distribution of religious groups. The subject and theme represent the author's interest, skills, political viewpoints, and historical context. Thus, maps represent only a version of reality. Maps are like snapshots of the world, a moment in time and space with a definite historical context. A nice example of perspective can be seen in one of the earliest known maps from the Babylonians. In this map the Babylonians are situated precisely in the middle of the universe; all the rest radiated from them—their own perception of the world. (We continue to see the world from our own perspective, of course, and this is reflected in our own maps.)

A world map from the sixteenth century shows the continents as far as the Europeans knew them during that age of discovery. Compare a sixteenth century map to any later chart of the Americas and note how different in size and shape the continents are at different periods of time (clearly, the continents themselves did not change that much, that quickly). The earlier world map reveals many things about the authors, not least of which is their knowledge of geography. One can see, from the examples of maps above, that the interest of the author is revealed by the selection of details for the map. The map would be rendered incomprehensibly complicated and useless. Nevertheless, maps are becoming more and more accurate. Cartographers, especially since the Late Middle Ages, have worked toward perfect map making.

This particular exercise book is designed to help you understand the relation between places and people through time. Maps and writing exercises are used to help you order events and historical locations. All sections incorporate several parts. Locate-and-label sections ask you to find and correctly place the number of a city, site or other feature or draw a boundary on the map. Geography-and-environment sections require you to become familiar with the natural context of a region. Human-society-and-civilization sections ask you interpret human interactions with other civilizations and with the natural world. You will need to relate and synthesize some historical and geographical information in a short-essay format. This workbook is intended to aid you in study and in the understanding of how events, people, and natural processes relate to one another temporally.

Bibliography

Demko, George with Jerome Agel and Eugene Boe. 1992. *Why in the World, Adventures in Geography*. New York: Doubleday. This is a fun and easy to read introduction to mapping and geography. It does an excellent job of pointing out the importance of geography.

Greenhood, David. 1964. *Mapping*. Chicago: University of Chicago Press. This book provides a clear and concise introduction to maps and mapping.

Harley, J. B. and D. Woodward (eds.). *The History of Cartography*. University of Chicago Press (in press). This work presents the history of maps and mapping in several volumes.

Talbert, Richard J. A. "Mapping the Classical World: Major Atlases and Map Series 1872-1990," *Journal of Roman Archaeology 5* (1992: 5-38). This article is especially interesting for students of ancient history.

Wood, Denis. 1992. *The Power of Maps*. New York: The Guilford Press. In this book Wood shows how maps are used and abused. It is an excellent introduction to the way maps have been used by groups and individuals to make an argument or present a point of view.

Useful Web Sites

http://www.pcclinics.com/maps/hist_sites.htm
http://maps.com
http://www.carto.com

Acknowledgements

I would like to thank the undergraduate students in the History of Western Civilization courses at Northern Arizona University. They provided indispensable help and advice in the development of my workbooks. I'd also like to thank Kevin Lawton, Arthur Lawton, Sibylle Gruber, Laura Gray-Rosendale, Jean Boreen and Randi Reppen for their editorial and content advice.

Section I: The World in Perspective — Introductory Exercises

Human Habitation Over Time

This exercise puts areas of human settlement over time into perspective. Using the four blank world maps located on pages 2-5, you will first chart human influence in global terms.

LOCATE AND LABEL

Map 1a: The earliest civilizations were found worldwide and were associated with the development of agriculture. People flourished in the hills and valleys of Mesoamerica, the Fertile Crescent, India, China and Egypt. On the map provided, shade in the areas across the globe that had developed agricultural civilizations by 2000 BCE.

Map 1b: On the map provided, shade in the areas across the globe that had developed agricultural civilizations by two-thousand years later at around 1 BCE / 1 CE.

Map 1c: On the map provided, shade in the areas across the globe that had developed agricultural civilizations by 1500 CE.

Map 1d: Finally, on the map provided, shade in the areas across the globe that presently have settled civilizations, leaving any unsettled territories blank.

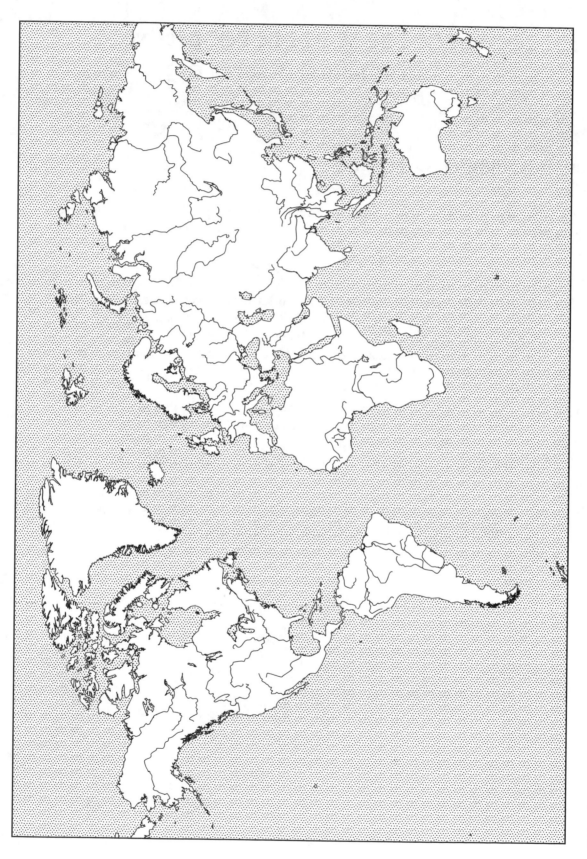

Map 1a

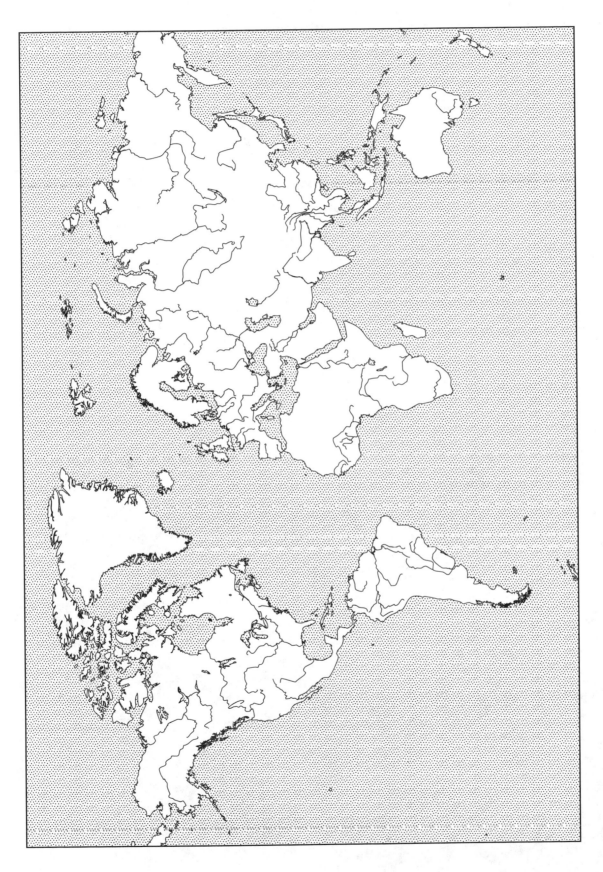

Map 1b

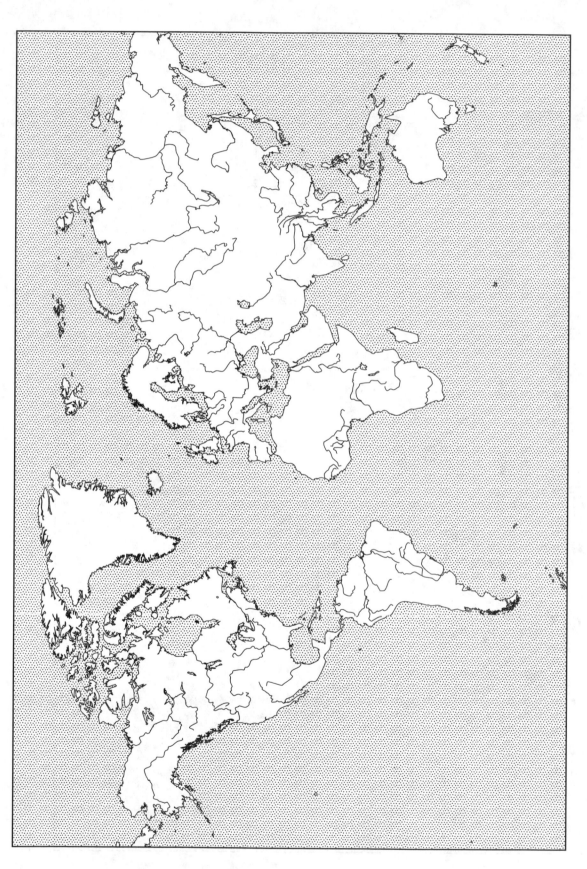

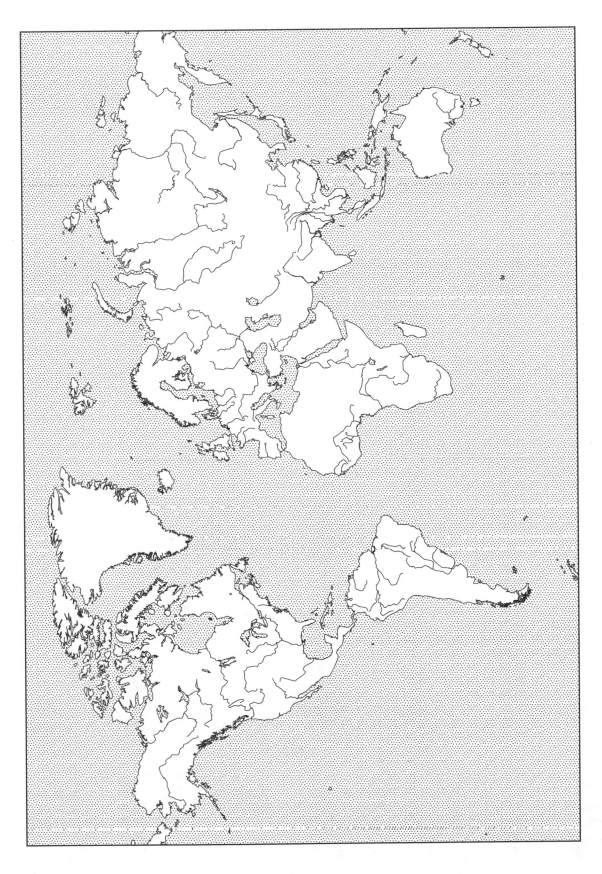

Map 1d

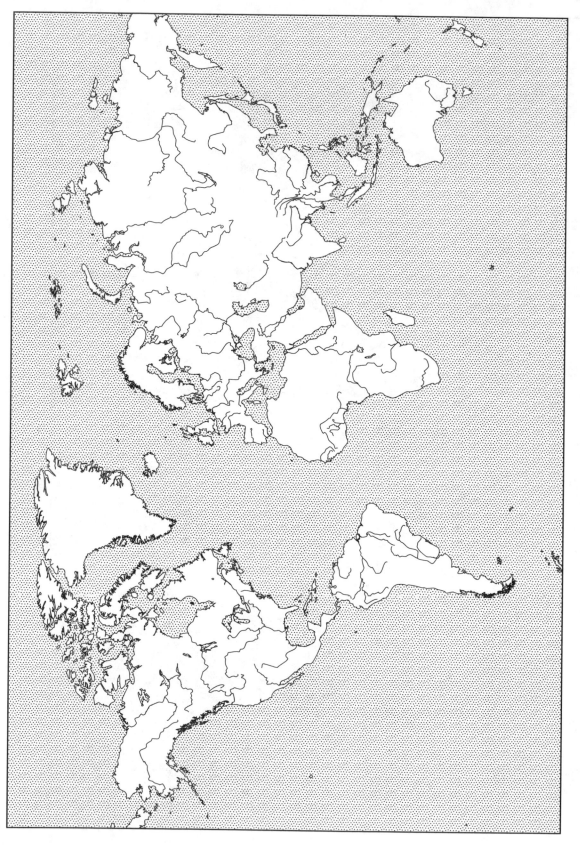

Map 2

Major Regions

This exercise puts the major regions of the planet, as we know them today, into perspective. Civilizations developed in a world context. They were not, and are not, isolated entities. Interactions among the various regions and people are evident from very early in human history. People traded with one another for food, tools and raw materials. In that process, they learned about one another, sometimes adopting practices, sometimes improving upon the technologies and customs that they found.

LOCATE AND LABEL

On Map 2, with different colored pencils, shade or draw in and number the following regions and geographical features. You may number the locations and place the numbers on the appropriate map for clarity.

A. Regions:
1. Anatolia
2. Arabia
3. Australia
4. Balkan Peninsula
5. Britain
6. China
7. Egypt
8. Fertile Crescent
9. Iberian Peninsula
10. Iran
11. Japan
12. North Africa
13. North America
14. Russia
15. South America
16. Southeast Asia

B. Rivers:
17. Amazon
18. Danube
19. Ganges
20. Mississippi
21. Nile
22. Rhine
23. Tigris
24. Yangtze

C. Seas, Oceans, Lakes:
25. Atlantic Ocean
26. Black Sea
27. Caribbean
28. Great Lakes
29. Indian Ocean
30. Mediterranean
31. North Sea
32. Pacific Ocean
33. Persian Gulf
34. Red Sea

D. Mountains:
35. Alps
36. Caucasus
37. Himalayans
38. Pyrennes
39. Rockies
40. Taurus

TEST YOUR UNDERSTANDING

1. How, when and why did agriculture develop?

    _____

    _____

    _____

    _____

    _____

    _____

    _____

2. What are the major theories used to explain the existence and development of civilizations?

    _____

    _____

    _____

    _____

    _____

    _____

    _____

    _____

    _____

3. What advantages and disadvantages do civilizations offer to us as human beings?

    _____

    _____

    _____

    _____

    _____

    _____

    _____

    _____

Section II: The First Civilizations and the Rise of Empires (to the Fourth Century CE)

Emergence of Civilizations and Empires in the Mediterranean and Near East

The first civilizations were found in the valleys of the Fertile Crescent, India, China and Egypt. Western civilization can be traced to the early societies of the Near East and Egypt. Mesopotamia, Greek for the "land between the rivers," was a rich land but difficult to farm. It took cooperation to build the irrigation systems needed to produce large quantities of agricultural goods. It was here that some of the earliest precursors to Western civilization were born. Writing, science, organized religion, and advanced technologies were a part of these civilizations.

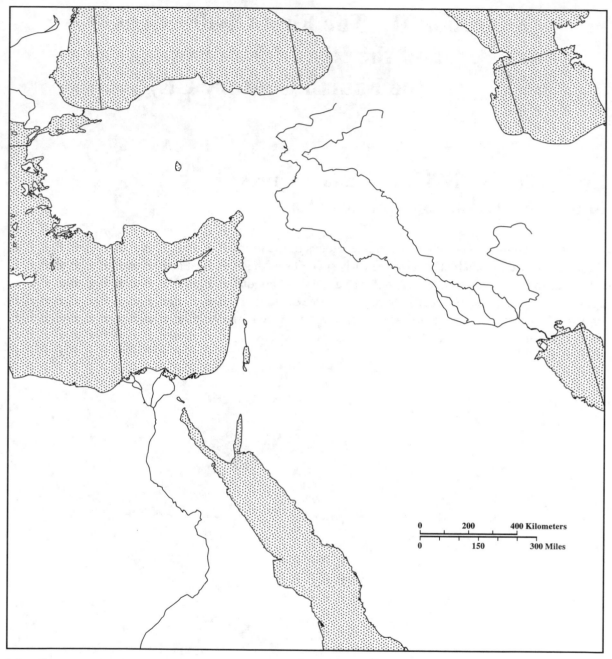

Map 3

Near East and Egypt

From the Near East and Egypt we also get some of the earliest complex civilizations, with organized religion, public works projects, and writing. The Hebrews, a small tribe of people, provide us with a spiritual heritage out of proportion to their size. Small states gave way to empires and these gave way to new states and imperial systems. These states grew up around cities. Thus, the Near East and Egypt are home to some of the oldest urban centers on earth.

LOCATE AND LABEL

With different colored pencils, place the number in the proper location and carefully shade in the regions and empires of the following peoples on the appropriate map. Also place the numbers of the following Near Eastern and Egyptian cities on the map.

A. Cities:	B. Empires:	C. Regions:	D. People:
1. Amarna	11. Assyrian	16. Akkad	28. Mitanni
2. Babylon	12. Chaldean	17. Asia Minor	29. Philistines
3. Çatal Hüyük	13. Egyptian	18. Assyria	30. Phoenicians
4. Giza	14. Hittite	19. Lower Egypt	
5. Jerusalem	15. Persian	20. Mesopotamia	
6. Lagash		21. Nile Delta	
7. Memphis (Egypt)		22. Parthia	
8. Nineveh		23. Persia	
9. Thebes (Egypt)		24. Sinai	
10. Uruk		25. Sumer	
		26. Syria	
		27. Upper Egypt	

SHORT ESSAY QUESTIONS

1. Based on your reading, compare briefly the physical environments of Çatal Hüyük and Babylon.

_____

_____

_____

_____

2. How do you think physical environment affected the religious and political beliefs of the settlers at Çatal Hüyük and Babylon?

_____

_____

_____

_____

3. Briefly discuss how the natural environment influenced the writing of the Mesopotamian creation myths and the *Epic of Gilgamesh*.

_____

_____

_____

_____

4. What political and religious factors made the Persians successful rulers of so many diverse peoples?

_____

_____

_____

_____

5. What attracted Persians and Assyrians to the shores of the Mediterranean?

_____

_____

_____

_____

6. Briefly describe the different peoples living in Palestine in the first millennium BCE.

_____

_____

_____

_____

7. In a short paragraph, compare the religion of the Hebrews with that of their neighbors. How did the local environment impact the nature of these religions?

_____

_____

_____

_____

_____

_____

8. From your reading describe the physical environment of the Nile Delta, and the cities of Thebes and Memphis.

_____

_____

_____

_____

9. What roles did the Nile and the Mediterranean play in the development of Egyptian society and economy?

_____

_____

_____

_____

10. How did the Egyptian natural environment affect the political beliefs and behaviors of the Egyptians?

_____

_____

_____

_____

11. How is the Egyptian natural environment reflected in their beliefs? Please be as specific as possible.

_____

_____

_____

_____

12. How did the natural environment of Egypt influence cultural developments? Please be as specific as possible.

_____

_____

_____

_____

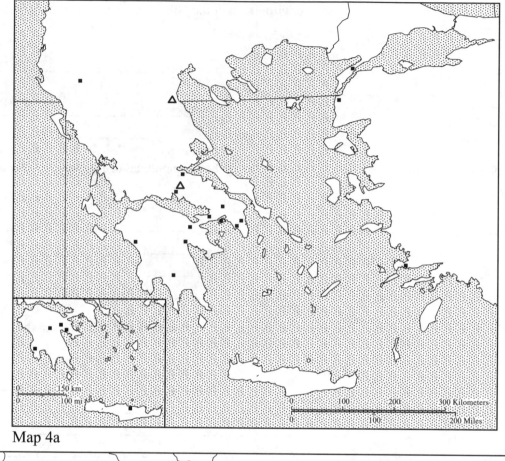

Map 4a

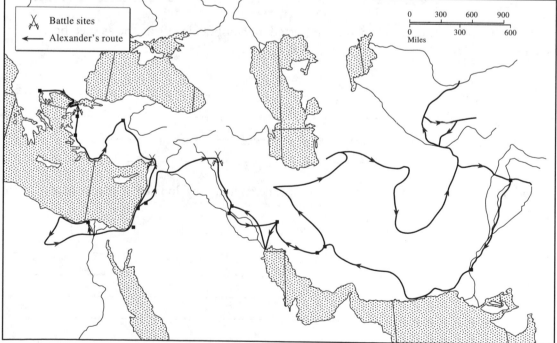

Map 4b

Empires in Greece and Macedon

The world of the ancient Greeks was divided up into many small city-states. Geography, especially the mountains and the sea, played an important role in their development. The islands of the Cyclades, which form a rough circle coming off the tip of Euboea and Attica, were inhabited very early. They were politically important for resources, military strategy and religion. Melos was the only local source of obsidian for weapons and surgical instruments. Delos was considered the home of Apollo and was sacred. On Crete an early Greek civilization flourished for more than a thousand years. Not infrequently the states of the mainland used and depended upon the political and economic support of these island people.

Empires in the region began with the conquests of the Athenians after the formation of the Delian League—which, though misused as a tool of expansion, was originally created as a defensive alliance of Greek states in opposition to the Persians. Alexander the Great elaborated on the imperial system begun by the Athenians and changed the political map of the "civilized" world. His ambitions led him to conquer his neighbors on the Balkan Peninsula and then head to the east. He incorporated dozens of cultures and thousands of miles into his Macedonian Empire. The creation of this empire was hard won, but not long lasting. Upon Alexander's untimely death, his conquests were divided among his faithful generals.

LOCATE AND LABEL

Label the most appropriate insert map to the left. With different colored marking pens or pencils, shade in and place the number in the appropriate location for the following regions or islands, geographical features, and cities.

A. Regions:
1. Asia Minor
2. Boeotia
3. Corcyra
4. Crete
5. Delos
6. Euboea
7. Ionia
8. Laconia
9. Lesbos
10. Macedonia
11. Melos
12. Naxos
13. Peloponnesus
14. Samos
15. Thera
16. Thessaly
17. Thrace

B. Geographical Features and Regions:
18. Aegean
19. Balkan Peninsula
20. Iberian Peninsula
21. Italy
22. Mt. Olympus
23. Nile River
24. Propontis
25. Sea of Crete

C. Cities:
26. Argos
27. Athens
28. Corinth
29. Cyrene
30. Ephesus
31. Knossos
32. Miletus
33. Mycenae
34. Olympia
35. Persepolis
36. Sparta
37. Susa
38. Thebes
39. Troy
40. Tyre

SHORT ESSAY QUESTIONS

1. What role did geography play in the evolution of Greek history?

    _____

    _____

    _____

    _____

    _____

    _____

2. How does the geography of Greece compare to that of Egypt and the Near East?

    _____

    _____

    _____

    _____

    _____

    _____

3. What advantages and what disadvantages did the Greeks have because of their geographical location?

    _____

    _____

    _____

    _____

    _____

    _____

4. Describe the areas associated with the Minoan and Mycenaean cultures and give their approximate dates.

    _____

    _____

    _____

    _____

    _____

    _____

5. The Greeks were rarely a quietly settled people. Using the discussion on colonization in your text, describe the areas settled by the Greeks and the Phoenicians and give the dates of settlement.

_____

_____

_____

_____

_____

6. When and where did the colonization movement begin?

_____

_____

_____

_____

_____

7. Why did the Greeks choose to colonize where they did?

_____

_____

_____

_____

_____

8. What human and environmental factors contributed to the successful campaigns of Alexander the Great?

_____

_____

_____

_____

_____

9. What were the long-term effects of Alexander's conquests on the areas that he captured?

_____

_____

_____

_____

_____

ESSAY

Life in Greece: Imagine that you are a foreign slave in Classical Athens. Write a brief essay about the circumstances that led to your enslavement, where you came from, and carefully describe the routes you traveled to arrive in Athens.

Imperialism Perfected: Rome and its Empire

The Romans forged one of the world's longest lasting imperial systems—in ancient or modern history. They created a legacy of conquest that we all share (whether we are the conquerors or conquered). It all began on the Italian peninsula in a little village on the banks of the Tiber River. After the conquest of the Italian peninsula, the Romans began to interact more aggressively with their more distant neighbors. Beginning in the western Mediterranean, the Romans gained territory rapidly and forcefully. Among the most famous of all the wars fought by the Romans were the Punic wars with the Carthaginians. One of the greatest Carthaginian generals was Hannibal—he was among the few who attacked the Romans on their own territory in these early days of Roman growth.

Despite internal social and political upheavals, the Romans managed to forge a strong and enduring political system. The Romans continued to expand their lands after an imperial system of government was in place. New territories were needed to bring in more income. As regions were added to the empire, the need for an efficient and regulated administration grew. Wisely, and whenever possible, the Romans co-opted existing systems of management. The Roman approach to control of subject people—allowing people to keep their languages, and usually their religions and political structures intact—tended to smooth the transition to membership in the empire and reduced the chances of rebellion and dissatisfaction.

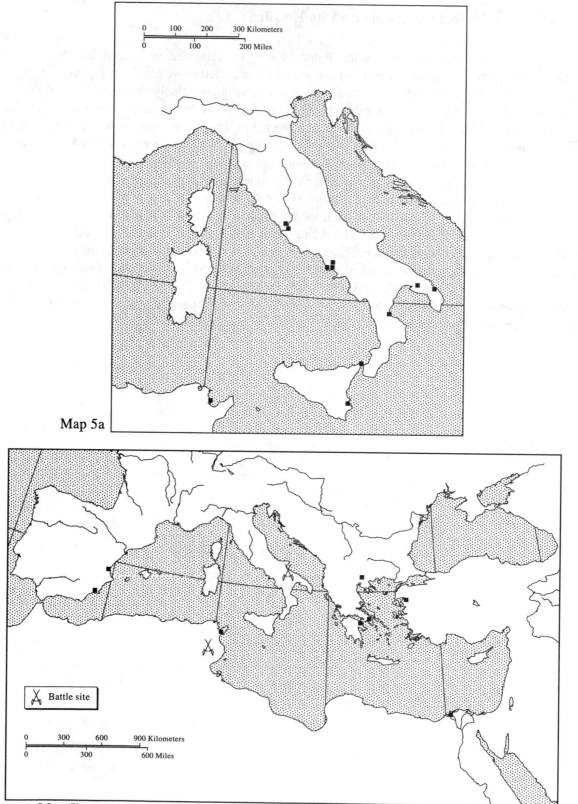

Map 5a

Battle site

Map 5b

LOCATE AND LABEL

With different colored marking pens or pencils, place the proper number in its location for the following cities, and approximately shade in and number the following regions and geographical features.

A. Cities and Battle Sites:
1. Brindisi
2. Cannae
3. Cumae
4. Cynoscephalae
5. Messina
6. Naples
7. Rome
8. Saguntum
9. Syracuse
10. Tarentum
11. Trasimene
12. Veii
13. Zama

B. Regions, Provinces and Frontiers:
14. Africa
15. Arabia
16. Asia
17. Britain
18. Carthage
19. Cisalpine Gaul
20. Dacia
21. Etruria
22. Greece
23. Illyria
24. Judaea
25. Latium
26. Macedonia
27. Magna Graecia
28. Numidia
29. Sardinia
30. Scotland
31. Sicily
32. Spain

C. Geographical Features:
33. Adriatic Sea
34. Apennine Mountains
35. Arno River
36. Po River
37. Rhône River
38. Rubicon River
39. Taurus Mountains
40. Tiber River

SHORT ESSAY QUESTIONS

1. What areas in Italy provided the best agricultural land?

_____

_____

_____

_____

2. What other resources did the peninsula provide for the Italians?

_____

_____

_____

_____

3. Compare the geography of Italy to that of the Greek peninsula.

    _____

    _____

    _____

    _____

    _____

    _____

4. What natural advantages did Italy possess over Greece and how did this affect their respective histories?

    _____

    _____

    _____

    _____

    _____

    _____

5. What were the main natural and man-made resources from Spain, Greece, Egypt, Sicily, and Northern Africa?

    _____

    _____

    _____

    _____

    _____

    _____

6. Why were the Romans interested in the western Mediterranean? The eastern?

    _____

    _____

    _____

    _____

    _____

    _____

7. Why were cities so important to the Romans? Describe the various functions that they served.

_____

_____

_____

_____

_____

_____

_____

8. What were the major differences between the cities of the eastern and western empire?

_____

_____

_____

_____

_____

_____

_____

9. How were the provinces and frontiers of the Roman Empire governed and protected?

_____

_____

_____

_____

_____

_____

10. What were the long-term effects of Roman rule on the provinces of the Western empire?

_____

_____

_____

_____

_____

_____

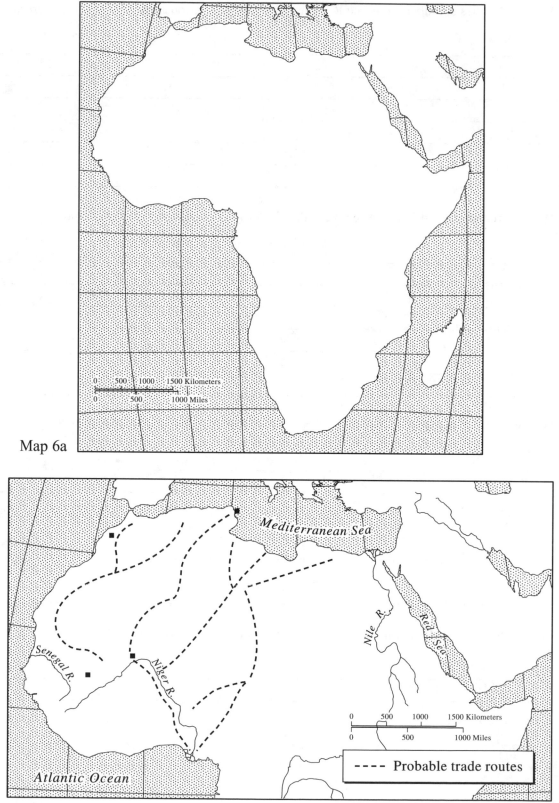

Map 6a

Map 6b

Emergence of Civilizations and Empires in Africa

Ancient Africa

Africa is the second largest continent on earth. It was home to the earliest hominids, the immediate ancestors to modern man, and arguably the site of the earliest cultivation of plants and domestication of animals (in Nubia). In Northern Africa, Egypt, of course, has long been recognized as one of the greatest of the world's early civilizations—by ancient, modern, eastern and western historians. Elsewhere in Africa, however, populous and complex states also appeared. A large variety of people inhabited this large continent and Africa provided an environment which inspired the creation of several distinct civilizations and kingdoms. This exercise introduces you to some of these people, their states, and some major geographical features.

LOCATE AND LABEL

On the map, label the following cities or settlements, people, regions, kingdoms and geographical features.

A. Cities or Settlements:
1. Adulis
2. Axum
3. Carthage
4. Marrakech
5. Meroe
6. Mombassa
7. Thebes
8. Timbuktu

B. People:
9. Berbers
10. Ghana
11. Hausa
12. Khoisan

C. Regions and Kingdoms:
13. Congo (or Kongo)
14. Egypt
15. Ethiopia
16. Kingdom of Kush
17. Madagascar
18. Nubia

D. Geographical Features:
19. Blue Nile
20. Congo River
21. Indian Ocean
22. Niger River
23. Nile River
24. Red Sea
25. Zambezi River

SHORT ESSAY QUESTIONS

1. Describe the locations and uses of the Iron Age sites found on the African continent.

_____

_____

_____

_____

_____

_____

2. What seems to have motivated people to live in these particular areas?

_____

_____

_____

_____

_____

3. What advantages and disadvantages would they have found in their environments?

_____

_____

_____

_____

_____

4. Briefly discuss the connections between the kingdoms of Kush, Axum and the western trading states. What kinds of items were exchanged?

_____

_____

_____

_____

_____

5. What were the long-term results of this trading activity?

_____

_____

_____

_____

_____

_____

Emergence of Civilizations and Empires in Asia

China

Ancient Chinese civilization began to emerge about 5,000 years ago along the Yellow and the Yangtze rivers. By the third century BCE, China had become a real empire and a dominant cultural and political force—as it remains today. This exercise considers some of the major geographical and cultural regions of early China.

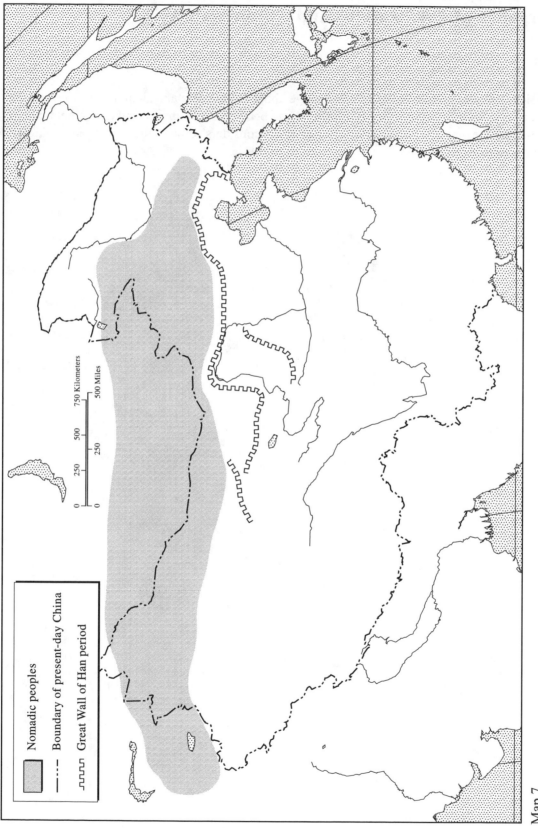

Map 7

LOCATE AND LABEL

With different colored marking pens or pencils, shade in and label the following cities, geographical features, regions and imperial boundaries in China.

A. Cities:
1. Anyang
2. Changan
3. Luoyang
4. Zhengzhou

B. Geographical Features:
5. Gobi Desert
6. Huai River
7. Pacific Ocean
8. South China Sea
9. Yangtze River
10. Yellow River
11. Yellow Sea

C. Empires and Regions:
12. Han Empire
13. Korea
14. Shang regions
15. Zhou Royal Domain

SHORT ESSAY QUESTIONS

1. Why are the two great rivers (Yellow and Yangtze) considered the core regions in the development of Chinese civilization?

_____

_____

_____

_____

_____

2. Along with written evidence, archaeological materials provide clues to early Chinese civilization. What, for example, do the excavations at Anyang reveal about the way the early Chinese lived?

_____

_____

_____

_____

_____

3. In what ways was the development of Chinese civilization the same, and in what ways was it different, from their contemporaries in Japan?

_____

_____

_____

_____

_____

4. In what ways was the development of Chinese civilization the same, and in what ways was it different, from their contemporaries in Africa?

_____
_____
_____
_____
_____
_____

5. In what ways was the development of Chinese civilization the same, and in what ways was it different, from their contemporaries in the Mediterranean?

_____
_____
_____
_____
_____
_____

Japan and Southeast Asia

Japan was inhabited from very early times. Though not at first as technologically skilled as its large neighbor to the west, China, the Japanese would create a vital, politically independent and culturally distinct society—as it remains to today.

Few Westerners know much about Southeast Asia, beyond the fact that the Vietnam War was fought in the region. This region was, however, home to one of the world's earliest bronze-age societies (in northern Thailand). Rice cultivation appeared perhaps as early as 9,000 years before the modern era.

The state of Srivijaya played a major role in commercial contact between China and India. In this area of Asia, there is an immense variety of races, cultures, and religions. This mixture is emphasized and increased because the region serves as a link between China, India and the islands of the South Pacific.

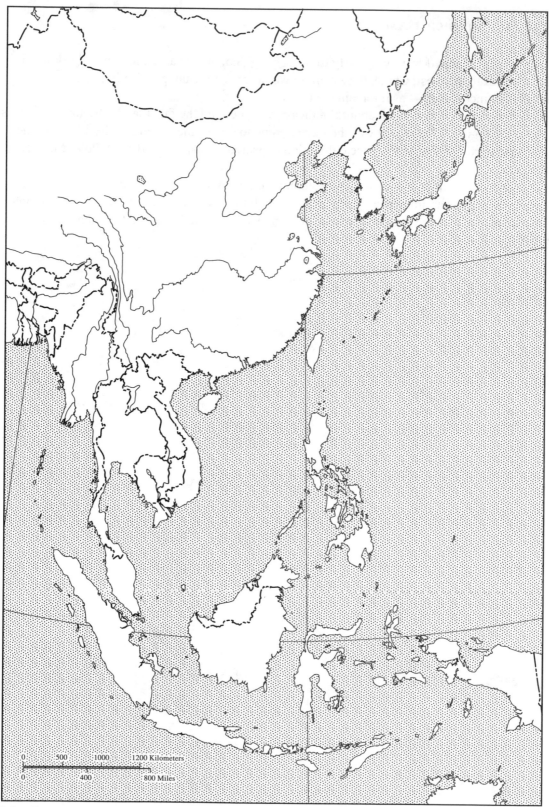

Map 8

LOCATE AND LABEL

With different colored pencils, shade in and label the following cities, geographical features and regions.

A. Cities:
1. Batavia
2. Borohudur
3. Canton
4. Indrapura
5. Kyoto
6. Macao
7. Malacca
8. Manila
9. Nara
10. Pagan
11. Palambag
12. Tali

B. Geographical Features and Regions:
13. Angkor
14. Borneo
15. Champa
16. China
17. Hokkaido
18. Japan
19. Korea
20. Malaya
21. Nan Chao
22. Okinawa
23. Pacific Ocean
24. Philippines
25. Shikoko
26. South China Sea
27. Srivijaya
28. Sumatra
29. Yellow River
30. Yangtze River

SHORT ESSAY QUESTIONS

1. What role did geography play in the development of Japan?

_____

_____

_____

_____

_____

_____

2. How does Japan's geographic environment differ from China's?

_____

_____

_____

_____

_____

3. What are the advantages and disadvantages of the Japanese environment?

    _____

    _____

    _____

    _____

    _____

    _____

4. Using a description of the geographical environment of the region, explain why Southeast Asia was never unified under a single government.

    _____

    _____

    _____

    _____

    _____

    _____

5. What trade goods were most important to the economies of the region?

    _____

    _____

    _____

    _____

    _____

    _____

Ancient India

The Indian subcontinent is large (roughly half the size of the United States) and is home to the world's tallest mountain range and the world's largest delta. India was also home to several early civilizations, which appeared in the region in about 3000 BCE. Most of what we know about the earliest of these comes from archaeological evidence rather than written records. Despite the lack of written records, diverse archaeological evidence shows that India has long been inhabited by vibrant and complex cultures.

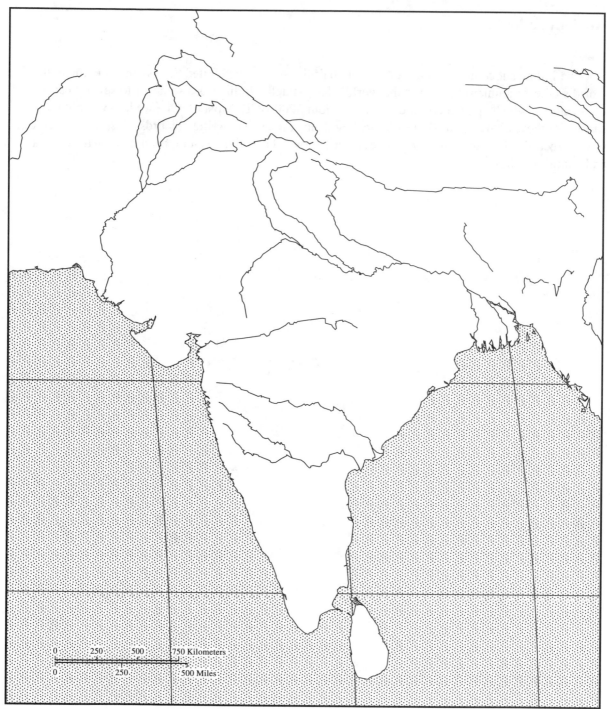

Map 9

LOCATE AND LABEL

Place the following features on the map provided.

A. Geographical Features and Regions:
1. Arabian Sea
2. Bactria
3. Bay of Bengal
4. Brahmaputra River
5. Ganges River
6. Gujarat
7. Himalayas
8. Indus River
9. Indian Ocean
10. Magadha
11. Sri Lanka

B. Cities:
12. Chanhu-Daro
13. Harappa
14. Lothal
15. Mohenjo-Daro

C. Routes:
With arrows, mark the approximate routes of the Indo-European invaders into India.

SHORT ESSAY QUESTIONS

1. Based on your reading, where did the first Indian civilization arise and why?

2. Briefly describe some of the similarities between the cultures of India and those of East Asia.

3. Briefly describe some of the differences between the cultures of India and those of East Asia.

4. What do the archaeological remains at Mohenjo-Daro tell us about Indian daily life?

_____

_____

_____

_____

_____

_____

_____

5. What factors seem to have caused the destruction of Mohenjo-Daro?

_____

_____

_____

_____

_____

_____

_____

Emergence of Civilizations and Empires in the Americas

The Early Americas

The Americas have long been inhabited by humans, but just how long is a matter of continued debate (perhaps since about 15,000 years ago). It is clear, however, that by the second millennium before the present era, highly organized societies had appeared in Central and South America. The civilizations that grew out of the smaller societies were characterized by vast trade networks, hierarchical political structures, written language, monumental architecture, and stunning and vivid artworks. This exercise is a brief introduction to the region and its major early tribes, chiefdoms and kingdoms.

Map 10

LOCATE AND LABEL

With different colored pencils, shade in and label the following.

A. Geographical Features,
City Centers and Regions:
1. Alaska
2. Amazon River
3. Andes Mountains
4. Atlantic Ocean
5. Caribbean Sea
6. Gulf of Mexico
7. La Venta
8. Mesoamerica
9. Pacific Ocean
10. Peru
11. San Lorenzo
12. Tres Zapotes
13. Yucatan Peninsula

B. Chiefdoms, States or Empires:
14. Aztec
15. Inca
16. Maya
17. North Andean Chiefdoms

C. Farming and Hunting Peoples:
18. Arctic littoral hunters
19. Savannah farmers
20. Woodland farmers

SHORT ESSAY QUESTIONS

1. The civilizations of the Americas developed in relative isolation from the rest of the world—undisturbed until the arrival of Columbus and the Spanish. What were the advantages and disadvantages of this isolation?

_____
_____
_____
_____
_____
_____

2. Discuss some of the cultural achievements made by the people of the Americas.

_____
_____
_____
_____
_____
_____

3. How did the Olmec centers come to prosper?

    _____

    _____

    _____

    _____

4. What do historians consider one of the greatest hindrances to further development among the Olmec?

    _____

    _____

    _____

    _____

5. What were the major crops and trade items among the people of the Americas? Be sure to distinguish these carefully by region.

    _____

    _____

    _____

    _____

    _____

6. Describe the natural environment around Teotihuacán.

    _____

    _____

    _____

    _____

7. What effect did the environment have on the creation of the huge city of Teotihuacán? Describe the lifestyle of the inhabitants.

    _____

    _____

    _____

    _____

    _____

8. What factors led to the rise of the Aztec Empire?

_____

_____

_____

_____

9. What technological skills did the Aztec introduce?

_____

_____

_____

_____

ESSAY

Compare and contrast the Aztec Empire to the Roman Empire. Why did the Aztec suffer more rebellions than the Romans?

_____

_____

_____

_____

_____

_____

_____

_____

_____

_____

_____

_____

_____

_____

_____

_____

_____

TEST YOUR UNDERSTANDING

A. For each of the following regions, list the major natural resources and manmade products available prior to 400 CE.

Asia Minor

_____

_____

England

_____

_____

Gaul/France

_____

_____

Italy

_____

_____

Spain

_____

_____

Central America

_____

_____

South America

_____

_____

India

_____

_____

Southeast Asia

_____

_____

China

_____

_____

B. For each of the following empires, briefly describe the territorial boundaries at their largest extent.

Assyrian Empire

_____

_____

Neo-Babylonian Empire

_____

_____

Empire of Alexander the Great

_____

_____

Roman Empire in the Late Republic

_____

_____

Qin Empire of China

_____

_____

Asoka Empire of India

_____

_____

C. Match the geographical, agricultural or archaeological features to the region with which it is most accurately associated.

___ 1.	Adriatic Sea	A.	Asia Minor
___ 2.	Alps	B.	Caribbean lowlands
___ 3.	Amazon River	C.	China
___ 4.	Coliseum	D.	Egypt
___ 5.	Great Wall	E.	Egypt/Arabian Peninsula
___ 6.	Taurus Mountains	F.	Gaul
___ 7.	Dead Sea	G.	Greece
___ 8.	Maize and manioc	H.	Israel
___ 9.	Nile	I.	Italy
___ 10.	Pyrennes Mountains	J.	Italy/Illyria
___ 11.	Red Sea	K.	Mesopotamia
___ 12.	Tiber	L.	Rome
___ 13.	Tigris	M.	South America
___ 14.	Pillar Edicts	N.	Spain
___ 15.	Parthenon	O.	India

Section III: New Patterns of Civilization to 1600

New Patterns in the Mediterranean and Near East

While the Roman political system dissolved in the western provinces and was replaced by smaller kingdoms, empires and principates, the Roman government in the East was stable, and despite some invasions and migrations was able to forge a long lasting Late Roman or "Byzantine" state. The Middle Ages, thus, developed very differently in the East and the West. The western regions were transformed by the influences of German, Celtic, Slavic and other traditions. The East, while not untouched by new ideas, maintained ancient Greek and Roman traditions, even in the face of strong Arab and Islamic pressure.

This Eastern Roman Empire has become known as the Byzantine Empire, though the people continued to consider themselves "Roman." The emperors of the East treated the Germans in the West as regents of Roman power. In the sixth century, however, an attempt was made to reunite the old empire into a territorial and institutional whole. The Emperor Justinian was the mastermind behind this plan, and he was partially and temporarily successful gaining territories as far west as Italy. Conflict, not unnaturally, resulted from diverse ideas of the nature and ownership of power in the West.

Conflict also occurred in the Near East, when in the seventh century Arab tribes began to accept a new religion, Islam, and to expand their influence in both the eastern and western Mediterranean world. The acceptance of Islam by the Arabs was rapid and complete. The reasons for such a rapid and successful religious revolution are still not clear. Upon unifying politically as well as religiously, the Arabs began to expand their territory.

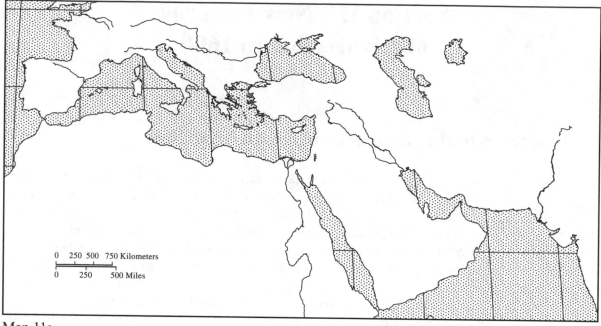

Map 11a

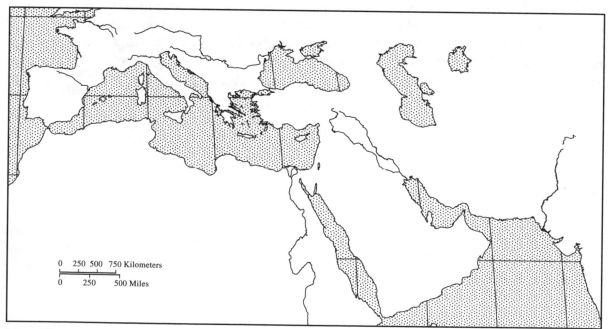

Map 11b

LOCATE AND LABEL

Since this "locate and label" map will be fairly full, take your time and place the locations carefully on your map. Two maps have been provided for easier completion of this assignment. Use Map 11a for parts A-C, and Map 11b for part D.

Place the following locations on Map 11a:

A. Cities and Sites:
1. Alexandria
2. Antioch
3. Baghdad
4. Carthage
5. Constantinople
6. Cordoba
7. Damascus
8. Jerusalem
9. Mecca
10. Medina
11. Poitiers
12. Rome
13. Tripoli
14. Tunis

B. Regions and Peoples:
15. Arabia
16. Bulgars
17. Egypt
18. Ostrogoths
19. Persians
20. Sahara Desert
21. Vandals
22. Visigoths

C. Geographical Features:
23. Caucasus Mountains
24. Euphrates River
25. Mediterranean Sea
26. Persian Gulf
27. Red Sea
28. Taurus Mountains

Lightly shade in and label the following state boundaries on your Map 11b. Use different colors to make identification of regions easier.

D. Territorial Boundaries:

29. Islamic Territories (ca. 632 CE)
30. Islamic Territories (ca. 661 CE)
31. Islamic Territories (ca. 750 CE)
32. Persian Empire (ca. 750 CE)
33. Byzantine Empire at the time of the Emperor Justinian
34. Byzantines (ca. 930 CE)
35. Byzantine (ca. 1452 CE)

SHORT ESSAY QUESTIONS

1. What were the material and environmental advantages of the territories held by Justinian?

_____

_____

_____

_____

2. Describe the major trade routes in the Byzantine Empire.

_____

_____

_____

_____

_____

_____

3. What, and from where, were the major goods being imported into Byzantium?

_____

_____

_____

_____

4. What were the major goods being exported from Byzantium?

_____

_____

_____

_____

5. What role did the location of Constantinople have on trade in the Byzantine Empire?

_____

_____

_____

_____

6. What were the main socio-political characteristics of the Byzantine Empire in the eighth century?
    Can you relate these characteristics to the geographical context of the Byzantine world?

_____

_____

_____

_____

_____

_____

7. What impact did geography have on the spread of Islam in the Middle East, Africa and Europe? Be specific.

_____

_____

_____

_____

_____

8. What social and political factors enabled the territorial expansion of Islam on such a large scale?

_____

_____

_____

_____

_____

9. What factors or events stopped the territorial expansion of Islam into Christian Europe?

_____

_____

_____

_____

_____

ESSAY

Using your texts and other sources, write an essay describing how the advent of Islam changed the roles of women in Arabic society. Be sure to clarify the status of women prior to the birth of Muhammad (ca. 570 CE). At the end of your essay, please properly cite the sources that you used.

_____

_____

_____

_____

_____

_____

_____

_____

Sources used:

New Patterns in the European Middle Ages

After a series of migrations and invasions, the Roman political system was weakened in the western provinces and in eastern Europe and was eventually replaced by numerous small Germanic and Slavic kingdoms. The Christian Church also benefited from the withdrawal of Roman power from the West. Some form of Christianity was accepted by most of the German people who gained the old Roman territories. Around the territories on each side of the Oder River, there was considerable intermixing of Germans with Slavs (which, incidentally, resulted in instability in Polish borders—an instability which characterized Poland well into the twentieth century).

The Frankish (Merovingian) kingdom controlled the old Roman province of Gaul for several centuries. This was a united Christian kingdom. By the seventh century, however, the kingdom was divided and beginning to weaken. Charles Martel, the mayor of the palace of Austrasia, gained power as a result. Among the most important of his actions was the defeat of the Muslims at Poitiers. But it was his son, Pepin, who, with the help of the Catholic church, would depose the Merovingians. Thus a new Frankish kingdom was born—that of the Carolingians. The son of Pepin, Charlemagne (or Charles the Great), was the most renowned and powerful of the leaders of the Carolingians.

0   200   400   600 Kilometers

0   200   400 Miles

Map 12

LOCATE AND LABEL

On the appropriate map, using different colors for each group, shade in the boundaries and number the territories of the new western kingdoms listed below. Also number and place on the map cities and geographical features listed below. Also, using different colors for each group, lightly shade in the territories of and number the following successor groups.

A. Kingdoms and Regions:
1. Alemanni
2. Austrasia
3. Bulgars
4. Burgundy
5. Celts
6. Franks
7. Lombards
8. Mercia
9. Neustria
10. Ostrogoths
11. Picts
12. Vandals
13. Visigoths

B. Cities:
14. Aachen
15. Belgrade
16. Bordeaux
17. Danzig
18. Leipzig
19. Nuremberg
20. Paris
21. Verdun

C. Byzantine Neighbors:
22. Alemanni
23. Bulgars
24. Burgundians
25. Ostrogoths

D. Geographical Features:
26. Adriatic Sea
27. Baltic Sea
28. Danube River
29. Ebro River
30. Rhine River

SHORT ESSAY QUESTIONS

1. How did the environment and geography of Europe contribute to the migrations and invasions of the Germanic, Gothic and Slavic peoples?

_____

_____

_____

_____

_____

2. What cultural characteristics of the Germans do you consider to have an environmental explanation?

_____

_____

_____

_____

_____

3. What were the main causes of friction between the ancient Italian peoples and their German rulers?

_____

_____

_____

_____

_____

_____

4. Describe the environmental difficulties encountered by the agricultural populations in the era of the Carolingians.

_____

_____

_____

_____

_____

_____

5. Describe the major trade routes of the Carolingians.

_____

_____

_____

_____

_____

_____

6. In the West, what were the long-term political and economic results of the Treaty of Verdun?

_____

_____

_____

_____

_____

_____

7. Describe the linguistic and cultural differences that were emerging in the divided territories of the Carolingian Empire.

_____

_____

_____

_____

_____

8. What nations would emerge from the Carolingian territories?

_____

_____

_____

_____

9. List at least five of the major regions of the Holy Roman Empire. Try to offer an explanation for these divisions of the Holy Roman Empire. Did they help or hinder stability in the empire? Explain.

_____

_____

_____

_____

_____

_____

_____

10. Describe the major changes in the European countryside from 1000-1300 CE. In particular, what were the changes in available farmland, technology, and climate?

_____

_____

_____

_____

_____

_____

_____

_____

ESSAY

Imagine that you are a merchant from Constantinople and that you are traveling to the Carolingian court. Write an essay describing what sorts of goods might you be trading and your impressions of daily life in Early Medieval Europe. Note especially the things that differ most dramatically from your own experiences in the East.

New Patterns in the Late Middle Ages to the Reformation

The Turkish people, led by the Ottomans, conquered the Byzantine Empire in 1453 with the capture of Constantinople. This was a tremendous victory and afterwards the Turks were intent on expanding west into Europe. They added vast tracts of lands to their wealthy empire. The Ottomans were very effective at forcing the Europeans to accept them as an equal power. They had a very intricate and effective government, with a strong and well-organized military.

In addition, the twelfth through the sixteenth centuries saw a myriad of rapid and profoundly influential developments. Technological transformations, the creation of universities, population fluctuations and the infusion of dramatically new ideas led to the foundations of modern religious divisions and systems of government. There were a variety of reasons for these changes, including but not limited to, new ways of thinking imported from the East though peaceful trade and the violence of the Crusades, dislocations caused by the Black Death, (which was a disaster of enormous magnitude), and conflicts within and surrounding the Catholic church.

State systems varied by region and era. For example, though in the fourteenth century Italy had a well-established system of city-state governments, often in conflict with one another. By the fifteenth century there were only a few, very powerful states left. They vied with one another for a variety of reasons, often calling on the Papacy or the Holy Roman Empire of the Germans to support their claims. Frequent warfare was the result, and unification of Italy was a long way away.

400 Miles

600 Kilometers

Map 13

LOCATE AND LABEL

Place the following locations on the map provided.

A. University Cities:
1. Bologna
2. Cambridge
3. Chartres
4. Durham
5. Mainz
6. Naples
7. Notre Dame
8. Oxford
9. Paris
10. Prague
11. Reims
12. Rome
13. Seville
14. Toledo
15. Vienna

B. Regions and States:
16. Duchy of Ferarra
17. Duchy of Milan
18. Duchy of Modena
19. Duchy of Savoy
20. Kingdom of Naples
21. Papal States
22. Republic of Florence
23. Republic of Lucca
24. Republic of Siena
25. Republic of Venice

SHORT ESSAY QUESTIONS

1. Briefly list five of the earliest major Universities with the date of their foundation.

_____

_____

_____

_____

_____

2. What were the origins of these schools? Why did schools arise in the locations that they did?

_____

_____

_____

_____

_____

_____

_____

_____

_____

3. What physical and educational characteristics did these early universities share?

_____

_____

_____

_____

4. Can you offer an explanation for why there were fewer universities in Spain than in France?

_____

_____

_____

_____

5. What effect did the humanist movement have on education and the locations of schools?

_____

_____

_____

_____

_____

6. How did the five major fifteenth-century powers in Italy come to dominate?

_____

_____

_____

_____

_____

7. What role did geography play in the development of these regional powers?

_____

_____

_____

_____

_____

8. Using Renaissance recipes and menus as guides, discuss how trade in Renaissance Italy affected the daily lives of the elite.

_____

_____

_____

_____

_____

9. The Black Death killed from 25 to 50 percent of the population of Europe. In some cases entire villages were wiped out. Some cities saw their populations reduced by more than half. The disaster had cultural, economic and religious results. Briefly describe the nature of the Black Death, outline its progress through Europe, and discuss European responses to the Black Death. What were some of the psychological and religious responses experienced by the inhabitants of Europe? Give specific examples.

_____

_____

_____

_____

_____

_____

_____

_____

_____

_____

_____

_____

_____

_____

_____

_____

ESSAY

Imagine that you are a student in Bologna. Write a letter to your parents describing your location and experiences. For example, what is the town like? What do you eat? What forms of entertainment do you enjoy? What are you wearing?

_____

_____

_____

_____

_____

_____

_____

_____

_____

_____

_____

_____

_____

_____

_____

_____

_____

_____

_____

_____

_____

_____

_____

_____

_____

_____

_____

_____

The Age of Discovery and Conquest

In 1492 a new era in world history was launched. Christian European adventurers took their ships in search of wealth, fame and new worlds to conquer and convert. These men provoked a transformation of Africa, Asia, the Americas and Europe itself. A ferment of ideas and scientific advances furthered European efforts to explore and dominate the entire world. The English, French, Spanish, Portuguese and Dutch all fanned out to conquer and colonize the old and New World. Discoveries and conquests of rich lands and people kept Europeans interested in the foreign travel and control. Settlements and ports were founded along the coasts of Africa. Across the Atlantic, the Spanish especially, established rich and vast empires, conquering and killing huge numbers of Amerindians in the process and then replacing these indigenous people with imported slave laborers from Africa.

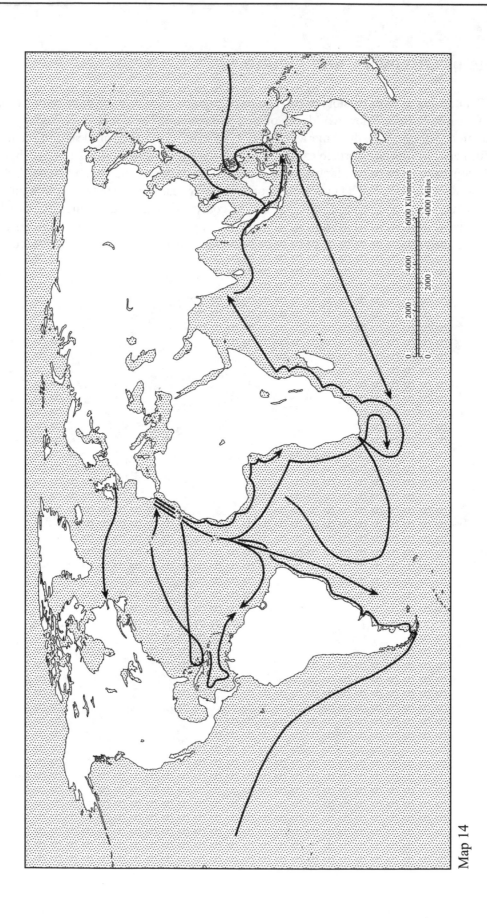

Map 14

LOCATE AND LABEL

On the map provided place the following locations and regions:

A. Regions:
1. Gold Coast
2. India
3. Japan
4. New Spain
5. Persia
6. Peru

B. Cities:
7. Bahia
8. Calicut
9. Elmina
10. Malacca
11. Manila
12. Mexico City
13. Mozambique
14. Nagasaki

C. Trade Routes (on the arrows indicate the routes and dates of the following explorers):
15. Cabot
16. Columbus
17. Da Gama
18. Dias
19. Magellan
20. Vespucci

SHORT ESSAY QUESTIONS

1. List and give the dates for the main voyages in the fifteenth and sixteenth centuries.

A) _____

B) _____

C) _____

D) _____

E) _____

F) _____

G) _____

H) _____

I) _____

2. What territories in the New World were under Spanish control by the sixteenth century?

_____

_____

_____

_____

3. What territories were under Portuguese control by the sixteenth century?

_____

_____

_____

_____

4. How were the New World territories administrated? Be sure to distinguish administrative practices by region.

_____

_____

_____

_____

_____

_____

5. What problems arose in the new territories because of the vast distances to the homelands?

_____

_____

_____

_____

_____

_____

New Patterns in Africa

The English, French, Spanish, Portuguese and Dutch all fanned out to conquer more than just the New World. People in Africa and Asia were also subject to influxes of these colonizers. Settlements and ports were founded along the coasts of Africa. After the Europeans had decimated huge numbers of Amerindians in the process of new world European settlement, they found a need for labor that could no longer be met locally. This fact resulted in the exploitation of African peoples and in particular the importing of slave laborers from the African continent.

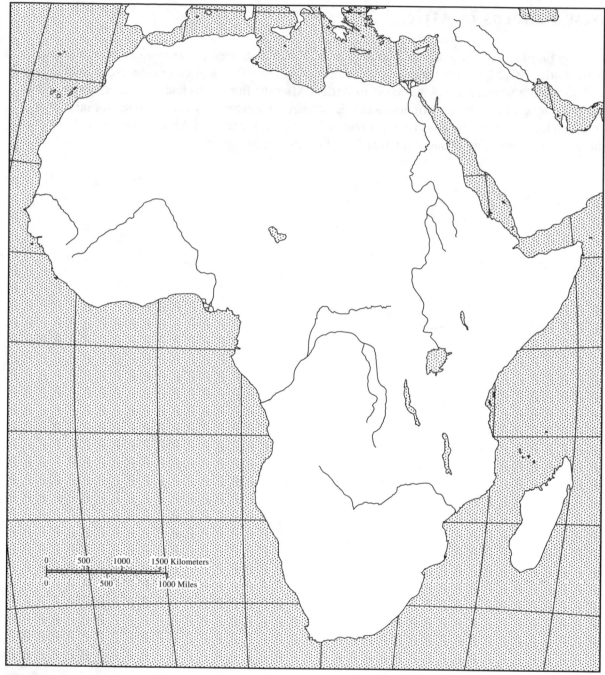

Map 15

LOCATE AND LABEL

Place or label the following locations on the map provided.

A. Geographical Features, Cities and Sites:
1. Atlantic Ocean
2. Cairo
3. Cape Town
4. Dakar
5. Kilwa
6. Mogadishu
7. Mombassa
8. Mozambique
9. Tunis
10. Zanzibar

B. Regions and States:
11. Angola
12. Congo (Kongo)
13. Ethiopia
14. Gold Coast
15. Slave coast

SHORT ESSAY QUESTIONS

1. Describe the general character of African political organizations. Consider west African organization in particular.

_____

_____

_____

_____

_____

2. From where in Africa did Europeans generally take people for enslavement?

_____

_____

_____

_____

_____

3. What effect did the slave trade have on the African states?

_____

_____

_____

_____

_____

4. Newly enslaved men and women were often taken to provide labor for the colonies in the New World. What effect did the slave trade have on these colonies?

_____

_____

_____

_____

5. Briefly discuss the connections between the kingdoms of Kush, Axum and the western trading states. What kinds of items were exchanged? What were the long-term results of this trading activity?

_____

_____

_____

_____

ESSAY

Timbuktu was founded in the twelfth century CE and still flourished by 1600. Briefly describe the city and its environs. What made Timbuktu important? How does the evidence from this site help us to understand state and cultural developments in Africa?

_____

_____

_____

_____

_____

_____

_____

_____

_____

_____

_____

_____

_____

_____

_____

_____

_____

New Patterns in Asia

India and Southeast Asia

Southeast Asia had long been a destination for traders and travelers because of its rich and varied resources. Politically and culturally the region was made up of many small groups. This fact made it relatively easy for European powers to establish control and to exploit the area's natural wealth.

In India, too, there were numerous political units. This left the Indians vulnerable to the powerful Moghul (also spelled Mughal) military dynasties. In the process of Moghul conquest, Hindu kingdoms were destroyed. Still, in an effort to reduce religious and cultural tensions, the new rulers pursued a policy of religious tolerance. That policy, however well intentioned, failed, and India was plagued with years of rebellions and religious conflicts. The Moghuls, however, effectively held off the European colonizers until the eighteenth century, and encouraged local arts and architecture, leaving behind beautiful monuments to their patronage. The Taj Mahal is one such monument.

East Asia

In 1368 the Chinese were finally able to overthrow Mongol rule. Civil and military collapse formed the backdrop for the emergence of strong indigenous Chinese empires. The Ming Dynasty first brought all of China under its control, and ultimately restored and rebuilt Chinese pride, arts, culture and economic life. Centuries later the last Ming Emperor left a shaky government and a rebellious population. Still, he left it to one of China's greatest rulers (Emperor K'ang-hsi, 1661-1722), the founder of the powerful Ch'ing (or Manchu) Dynasty.

Japan, in the sixteenth century, suffered a long series of civil wars, from which would emerge a unified and powerful state. Despite political unrest, trade flourished and agriculture expanded. Once political stability was achieved, Japan became isolationist and closed its ports to Europeans and thus enjoyed centuries of peace and prosperity.

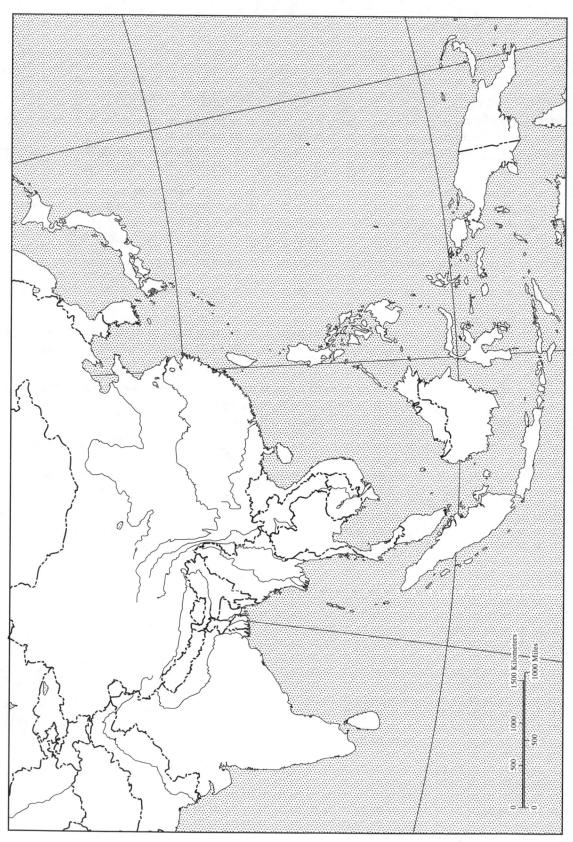

Map 16

LOCATE AND LABEL

Place the following cities, regions and geographical features on your map.

A. Geographical Features:
1. Bay of Bengal
2. East China Sea
3. Indian Ocean
4. Sea of Japan
5. South China Sea
6. Yellow Sea

B. Cities and Sites:
7. Batavia
8. Bombay
9. Calcutta
10. Canton
11. Delhi
12. Hanoi
13. Madras
14. Malacca
15. Manilla
16. Nagasaki
17. Nanking

C. States and Regions:
18. Bengal
19. Borneo
20. Cambodia
21. Ceylon
22. Japan
23. Java
24. Korea
25. Kyushu
26. Laos
27. Mysore
28. New Guinea
29. Philippines
30. Shikoki
31. Siam
32. Taiwan
33. Tibet
34. Timor
35. Vietnam

SHORT ESSAY QUESTIONS

1. What sorts of goods were produced by the people of the Southeast Asian islands? Where were these goods primarily traded?

_____

_____

_____

_____

_____

2. Describe the factors that led to the inability of the Portuguese to hold onto their commercial empire in Asia. Who replaced the Portuguese?

_____

_____

_____

_____

_____

3. Briefly describe the complex religious situation in India. What long-term impact has this complexity had on political and territorial stability?

_____

_____

_____

_____

_____

_____

4. Compare and contrast the environments of the Ming Empire at its largest extent, with the Ch'ing Empire at its largest extent. How did the environment affect their systems of government?

_____

_____

_____

_____

_____

_____

_____

5. What problems existed at the end of Mongol rule in China that encouraged Chinese uprisings?

_____

_____

_____

_____

_____

_____

_____

_____

_____

New Patterns in the Americas

With the conquest of the Americas by the Europeans, a new era began. European powers claimed these territories for themselves, regardless of the original inhabitant's desires. Europeans brought with them a new way of life and old conflicts. It took hundreds of years to sort out these conflicts fought on American soil. Moreover, a ferment of ideas and scientific advances furthered European efforts and desires to explore and dominate the entire world. The Spanish, Portuguese, Dutch, British and French, in particular, fanned out to claim parts of the globe that interested or benefited them. (By the early eighteenth century, for example, millions of Europeans lived in the Americas.) These newcomers, under the influence of the indigenous populations, developed new forms of Western culture.

Map 17

LOCATE AND LABEL

Place the following locations on the map provided.

A. Geographical Features and Islands:
1. Amazon River
2. Caribbean Sea
3. Colorado River
4. Cuba
5. Great Lakes
6. Gulf of Mexico
7. Mississippi River
8. Pacific Ocean
9. Rio Grande
10. Rocky Mountains

B. Cities and Sites:
11. Acapulco
12. Baltimore
13. Boston
14. Montreal
15. New Orleans
16. Panama
17. Quebec
18. Rio de Janeiro
19. Santa Fe
20. Sao Paulo
21. Veracruz

C. States and Regions:
22. Belize
23. Brazil
24. Canada
25. Guiana
26. Honduras
27. New Granada
28. New Spain
29. Peru
30. Yucatan

SHORT ESSAY QUESTIONS

1. What were some of the greatest differences between the old western European culture and the culture that developed in Latin America? Describe some of the innovations of the new Spanish-American culture.

2. Compare and contrast Latin American culture with the culture of British North America.

3. What explains European military successes over the indigenous societies?

_____

_____

_____

_____

_____

_____

4. By what means and for what reasons did the new United States of America free itself from British rule? How was this move similar and different from developments in Canada?

_____

_____

_____

_____

_____

_____

ESSAY

Write an essay discussing the short- and long-term impacts of European settlement on the people and environment of the New World. What impact did the discovery of these territories have on the countries and people of Europe?

_____

_____

_____

_____

_____

_____

_____

_____

_____

_____

TEST YOUR UNDERSTANDING

A. Next to the list of regions and cities, please write in the proper associated religion and the approximate date of conversion to that religion. Where the region underwent more than one conversion (e.g. from pagan, to *pre Reformation* Christian to Muslim) you will need to list all major conversions and their dates.

Aachen   _____

Alexandria   _____

Antioch   _____

Canterbury   _____

Cologne   _____

Cordoba   _____

Ephesus   _____

Fez   _____

Marseilles   _____

Mecca   _____

Medina   _____

Milan   _____

Nicaea   _____

Paris   _____

Tours   _____

B. Name at least five major centers of Christian diffusion in the western territories. Describe the locations of these centers and give an explanation for their importance.

_____

_____

_____

_____

_____

_____

_____

_____

_____

_____

_____

_____

_____

C. In the sixth and seventh centuries the Latin Christian church gained considerable power and prestige. Give at least two reasons why this was so.

_____

_____

_____

_____

_____

_____

_____

_____

_____

_____

    With respect to the Christian church, in the sixteenth century abuses by the Catholics, in particular the papacy, were reaching a crisis point. Many reform movements grew out of the frustration of the times, some made surprisingly influential by the dissemination of these new ideas through the written word, now easily spread because of the printing press. The Reformation in Germany led by Martin Luther was to be one of the most influential. It was not long before the population of Europe had chosen sides: Protestant (e.g. Lutheran, Calvinist, Anglican) or Catholic.

D. Next to the following cities, list the appropriate *post Reformation* religious affiliation (Anglican, Calvinist, Calvinist influenced, Roman Catholic, Lutheran, Lutheran influenced).

Amsterdam   _____

Cologne   _____

Dijon   _____

Edinburgh   _____

Geneva   _____

London   _____

Madrid   _____

Oxford   _____

Paris   _____

Rome   _____

Seville   _____

Trent   _____

Vienna   _____

Wittenberg   _____

Worms   _____

1. Compare and contrast the Reformation in England and Germany. How did local conditions affect the different approaches to reformation?

_____

_____

_____

_____

_____

_____

_____

_____

_____

_____

_____

_____

_____

2. What impact did the Reformation generally have on the economy of Europe? Give several examples.

_____

_____

_____

_____

_____

_____

_____

_____

_____

_____

_____

_____

_____

3. What impact did the Reformation have on the political life and territorial boundaries of Europe? On the other hand, what impact did existing territorial divisions have on the progress of the Reformation?

_____

_____

_____

_____

_____

_____

_____

_____

_____

_____

_____

_____

_____

4. What impact did the Reformation have on the society of Europe? Give several examples.

_____

_____

_____

_____

_____

_____

_____

_____

_____

_____

_____

_____

_____